# Cats vs. Dogs

Elizabeth Carney

**NATIONAL GEOGRAPHIC**

Washington, D.C.

For the McNally family, who has lovingly accepted me into their pack
—E.C.

**Library of Congress Cataloging-in-Publication Data**
Carney, Elizabeth, 1981-
Cats vs. dogs / by Elizabeth Carney. -- 1st ed.
p. cm.
Includes index.
ISBN 978-1-4263-0755-3 (pbk. : alk. paper) -- ISBN 978-1-4263-0756-0 (library binding : alk. paper)
1. Cats--Juvenile literature. 2. Dogs--Juvenile literature. I. Title. II. Title: Cats versus dogs.
SF446.5.C383 2011
636.8--dc22
2010037791

cover, John Lund; 1, Tim Davis/ Corbis; 2 (left), Anna Utekhina/ Shutterstock; 2(right), Anna Utekhina/ iStockphoto.com; 4, Sharon Montrose/ The Image Bank/ Getty Images; 5, Daniel Bobrowsky/ iStockphoto.com; 6, Mauricio Anton/ NationalGeographicStock.com; 7 (top left), Ian McAllister/ Canopy/ Corbis; 7 (center left), Tom Murphy/ NationalGeographicStock.com; 7 (bottom left), Steve Allen/ The Image Bank/ Getty Images; 7 (right), Pavel Shlykov/ iStockphoto.com; 8 (left), Anna Utekhina/ iStockphoto.com; 8 (top right), Art Wolfe/ The Image Bank/ Getty Images; 8 (center right), lightpoet/ Shutterstock; 8 (bottom right), Oksana Samuliak/ iStockphoto.com; 9 (top right), Natthawat Wongrat/ iStockphoto.com; 9 (center right), Kristian Sekulic/ iStockphoto.com; 9 (bottom right), Ken Klotz/ iStockphoto.com; 10 (top), Tracy Hebden/ iStockphoto.com; 10 (bottom), Digital Vision/ Photodisc/ Getty Images; 11 (top), Chris Bence/ iStockphoto.com; 11 (bottom), mage Source/ Getty Images; 11 (center), Anna Utekhina/ Shutterstock; 12 (top), Michael Blann/ Stone/ Getty Images; 12 (bottom left), Jani Bryson/ iStockphoto.com; 12 (bottom right), Deborah Bardowicks/ Photolibrary/ Getty Images; 13 (left), Anna Utekhina/ iStockphoto.com; 13 (right), Anna Utekhina/ iStockphoto.com; 14, Jane Burton/ Dorling Kindersley/ Getty Images; 15 (top), Iztok Noc/ iStockphoto.com; 15 (bottom), Anna Utekhina/ Shutterstock; 16, Moggy/ Stone/ Getty Images; 17 (left), Anna Utekhina/ iStockphoto.com; 17 (top right), Richard Ellis/ Getty Images; 18, Dorling Kindersley/ Getty Images; 19 (top), Dorling Kindersley/ Getty Images; 19 (bottom), Dave King/ Dorling Kindersley/ Getty Images; 20, Jean Frooms/ Shutterstock; 21 (top), Bloomimage/ Corbis; 21 (bottom), Michael Kloth/ Corbis; 22, Michael Kloth/ Corbis; 23 (top left), Sue Mack/ iStockphoto.com; 23 (top right), junku/ Flickr/ Getty Images; 23 (center left), Franz Aberham/ Stock Image/ Getty Images; 23 (bottom right), ILonika/ Shutterstock; 23 (bottom left), Ryerson Clark/ iStockphoto.com; 24 (top), John Giustina/ Taxi/ Getty Images; 24 (bottom), Anna Utekhina/ Shutterstock; 25 (top left), brandi ediss/ Flickr/ Getty Images; 25 (top right), Tom and Steve/ Flickr/ Getty Images; 25 (center left), Simone Mueller/ Taxi/ Getty Images; 25 (bottom right), Claudio Arnese/ iStockphoto.com; 25 (bottom left), Micheal Simpson/ Taxi/ Getty Images; 26 (top left), Tina Rencelj/ iStockphoto.com; 26 (center left), Martin Ruegner/ Workbook Stock/ Getty Images; 26 (center right), Rick Hyman/ iStockphoto.com; 26 (bottom left), Jason Edwards/ NationalGeographicStock.com; 26 (bottom right), Stephen Coburn/ Shutterstock; 27 (top left), Paulo De Oliveira/ Photolibrary/ Getty Images; 27 (top right), Sharon Dominick/ iStock Exclusive/ Getty Images; 27 (center left), Axel Lauerer/ Flickr/ Getty Images; 27 (center right), Vincent J. Musi/ NationalGeographicStock.com; 27, Jeffery R. Werner/ IncredibleFeatures.com; 28-29, ifong/ Shutterstock; 30 (top), Sean Russell/ fstop/ Corbis; 30 (bottom), Tatiane Noviski Fornel/ Flickr/ Getty Images; 31 (top), GK Hart/Vikki Hart/ Stone/ Getty Images; 31 (bottom left), Mecky/ Photonica; 31 (bottom center), Robert F. Sisson/ National Geographic/ Getty Images; 31 (bottom right), Dave King/ Dorling Kindersley/ Getty Images; 32, Dorling Kindersley/ Getty Images; 33, Alison Wright/ NationalGeographicStock.com; 34, David Joel/ Photographer's Choice RF/ Getty Images; 35, Mans, U./ plainpicture/ Corbis; 37 (top), image100/ Corbis; 37 (center left), GK Hart/Vikki Hart/ The Image Bank/ Getty Images; 37 (center right), ULTRA.F/ Digital Vision/ Getty Images; 37 (bottom), Photodisc/ Getty Images; 38 (top), iStockphoto.com; 38 (center left), Anna Utekhina/ iStockphoto.com; 38 (center right), Sharon Dominick/ Photodisc/ Getty Images; 38 (bottom), Tracy Morgan/ Dorling Kindersley/ Getty Images; 39 (bottom), Nataliya Kuznetsova/ iStockphoto.com; 39 (bottom left), Photodisc/ Getty Images; 40, Don Farrall/ Photodisc/ Getty Images; 41 (top), Tom Bear/ Aurora/ Getty Images; 41 (bottom), Marcel Jancovic/ Shutterstock; 42 (top), Chip East/ Reuters/ Corbis; 42 (bottom), Creativ Studio Heinemann/ Westend61/ Corbis; 43, Don Mason/ Brand X Pictures/ Getty Images; 44, Marina Maslennikova/ iStockphoto.com; 45 (top), Marilyn Conway/ Photographer's Choice RF/ Getty Images; 45 (bottom), Thomas Tolstrup/ Taxi/ Getty Images; 46 (top right), Steve Allen/ The Image Bank/ Getty Images; 46 (center right), Robert Clark/ NationalGeographicStock.com; 46 (bottom right), Pavel Shlykov/ iStockphoto.com; 46 (top left), cynoclub/ Shutterstock; 47 (bottom left), Eduard Kyslynskyy/ Shutterstock; 47 (top right), Nancy Nehring/ iStockphoto.com; 47 (top left), Wolfgang Steiner/ iStockphoto.com; 47 (bottom right), shadow216/ Shutterstock; 47 (center left), Kristian Sekulic/ iStockphoto.com; 47 (center right), Ocsi Balázs/ Shutterstock

Printed in the U.S.A.
12/WOR/3

# Table of Contents

# Cats vs. Dogs!

Dogs and cats are the most popular pets in the world. Some people think dogs are our finest friends. Others believe cats are the purr-fect pets.

Find out which animal has the smoothest moves, the best hearing, and can do the smartest tricks. No matter who your favorite is, one thing is certain: Fur will fly in this battle of the pets!

# Who has the scariest relatives?

Dogs and cats may seem like opposites. That's because they have very different family trees.

Millions of years ago, a foxlike predator prowled the plains hunting for meat. This animal, called *Eucyon davisi* (U-see-on dah-vee-see), was an early relative of the canines we see today.

Extinct dog ancestor Eucyon

Modern day gray wolf

wolf

dogs

coyote

Wolves, coyotes, jackals, and dogs are all related to this ancestor. These animals hunt and live in packs in the wild.

jackal

All cats, from the mighty tiger to the common house cat, evolved from a small, catlike creature that lived 12 million years ago. This animal was called *Felis attica* (Fell-ees ah-tik-ah).

**weird but true**

Big cats like lions, tigers, and jaguars can't purr like small cats do.

**Pet Words**

EVOLVE: To change or develop naturally over long periods of time

FELINE: A group of meat-eating mammals that includes the domestic cat, lion, tiger, lynx, and cheetah

puma

lynx

house cat

Later, the feline family split into two groups. One group evolved into smaller cats like pumas, lynxes, and house cats. The other evolved into big cats like tigers, lions, and leopards. Big cats are some of the world's most fearsome predators.

In a head-to-head battle, a wolf would be no match for a lion or tiger.

**WINNER:** cats!

tiger

lion

leopard

# Senses

## Whose nose knows best?

Dogs and cats have super sensing powers that have been passed down from their ancestors. Powerful senses have helped them survive.

**weird but true**

Some dog breeds can sniff out mold, insects, drugs, and even cancer. Now that's a knowing nose!

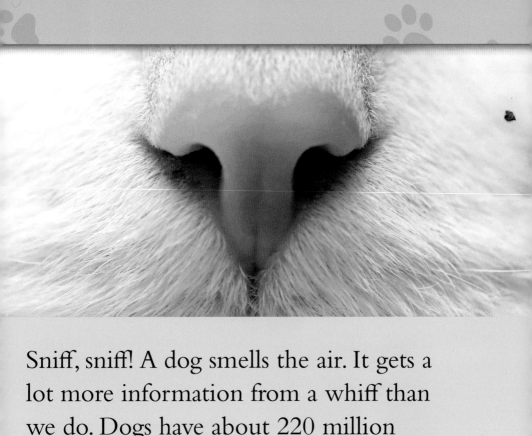

Sniff, sniff! A dog smells the air. It gets a lot more information from a whiff than we do. Dogs have about 220 million scent cells. That's twice as many as cats—and 40 times more than humans!

**Pet Words**

CELL: The basic building block of a living thing. Large plants and animals are made up of trillions of cells.

**WINNER: dogs!**

## Who's got an ear for everything?

A mouse scurries inside a hole in the wall. A human may not have heard a sound, but a passing cat probably did.

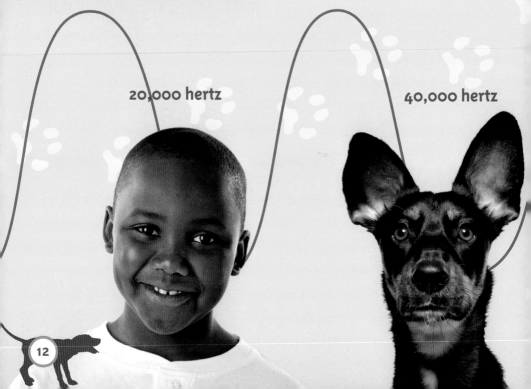

20,000 hertz

40,000 hertz

Humans can hear sound up to 20,000 hertz, a measurement of how high or low pitched a sound is. Dogs can hear twice that. But cats' hearing is king. They can pick up an ear-splitting 60,000 hertz! This means cats hear many sounds that humans and even dogs would never notice.

**WINNER: cats!**

**Pet Words**

HERTZ: A unit of measurement for sound

60,000 hertz!

# Diet

## Who serves up supper?

House cats are deadly hunters. Sometimes cat owners will open their front door and find a surprise: a dead animal! Cats often bring home "gifts" to their owners, like birds, lizards, or mice that they've killed.

**WINNER: cats!**

You might have preferred a pizza, but your cat is just following its instincts. Dogs might bring home the newspaper, but cats bring home dinner fit for a feline.

Pet Words

INSTINCT: Behavior that animals are born knowing how to do

## Who's a pickier eater?

Dogs and cats usually eat pet food that's specially made for them.

WINNER: cats!

In the wild, cats are carnivores. They eat only meat. Cats need five times more protein than do dogs.

Dogs are carnivores, too, but pooches aren't as picky. In the wild, dogs and wolves sometimes snack on plant matter like grass and fruit.

### Pet Words

**CARNIVORE:** An animal that eats other animals

**PROTEIN:** A nutrient in meat that is an important part of all living things

17

# Communication

## Who has a tattle tail?

Both cats and dogs show how they're feeling with their tails.

When cats hold their tails straight up, they're happy to see you.

18

A twitchy tail means a cat is ready to pounce.

Cats sweep their tails from side to side when they're feeling excited or aggressive.

Happy dogs wag their tails from side to side or round and round like a propeller.

When dogs are scared, they tuck their tail between their legs. If dogs are unsure about something, they keep their tails low and wag them close to their bodies.

Dogs hold their tails still and upright when they sense danger. This means trouble might be coming.

So who's the best at telling more tales with their tails? Dogs have more ways of using their tails to communicate than cats.

**WINNER: dogs!**

weird but true

A frightened dog tucks its ears down and hunches its back to appear smaller.

21

## Who's the chattiest?

Dogs and cats don't use words, but they have a wide range of sounds to tell how they're feeling.

Consult this cat dictionary to see what your cat is trying to tell you.

# CAT DICTIONARY

**Purr:** This sound signals kitty happiness. It means a cat is feeling comfortable and safe.

**Meow:** Cats have different meows that say many things. Each sound can have a different meaning, like "feed me," "pet me," or "hey there!"

**Yowl:** Some cats make a long wailing sound to get the attention of their owners or other cats.

**Hiss:** This is the sound cats make when trying to defend themselves. They raise their upper lips to show their teeth and blow out a jet of air.

**Growl:** This low sound made in the back of a cat's throat means "Stay away!"

Dogs have a wide range of sounds to "say" what's on their minds. Don't speak dog? This dog dictionary can help.

**weird but true**

Wolves howl to communicate with pack members or to give warnings to rival packs.

Dogs are related to animals that live in packs. Communication is an important part of pack life. Dogs need to use these sounds frequently to "chat" with other pooches or their owners.

**Pet Words**

PACK: A group of canines that lives and hunts together

# DOG DICTIONARY

**Whine:** Puppies give this high-pitched distress call if they're alone or hungry. It tells Mom to come help. Adult dogs whine to express pain or fear.

**Yip:** Dogs make this sound when feeling playful or when they want attention.

**Bark:** Dogs bark when they're bored, excited, or trying to find other dogs. They also use this sound to warn of strangers approaching.

**Howl:** Dogs howl when they are lonely or to make contact with family members.

**Growl:** When dogs make this sound with their ears held back, they're usually upset, tense, or angry.

WINNER: dogs!

# 10 Cool Things About Dogs and Cats

**1** A tiger can take down a 600-pound deer with a deadly bite to the throat.

**3** Dogs can drink muddy water and eat rotten meat or garbage without getting sick. Chemicals in a dog's stomach kill the germs.

**2** When domestic cats hunt mice, about one in three pounces results in a catch.

**4** Lions are the only cats that live and hunt in large groups.

**5** Dogs have six puppies per litter on average, but large breeds can have as many as 12 puppies.

**6**

A wolf can "wolf" down 20 pounds of meat in one sitting.

**7**

When a cat grooms itself, it removes dead hair and skin. Grooming also spreads the cat's scent and feels relaxing.

**8**

With their keen hearing ability, cats can tell when disasters like earthquakes and volcanic eruptions are about to occur.

**9**

A border collie named Betsy understands more than 340 spoken words. Betsy learns words as quickly as a small child.

**10**

A Great Dane named George holds the record as the tallest dog. Standing on his hind legs, George is over seven feet tall from head to tail.

# Behavior

## Who's the bigger sleepyhead?

Dogs sleep 12 hours a day on average. Older dogs or puppies might sleep more. Working breeds like boxers and collies don't need as much shut-eye.

Cats sleep about 18 hours a day. But unlike humans, cats sleep lightly, waking up every several minutes. That's where the term "catnap" comes from.

**WINNER: cats!**

## Who's the cleanest?

Cats spend over half their time licking themselves. A cat's tongue is rough like sandpaper. It's covered with backward-facing spines that turn the tongue into a mini-brush.

WINNER: cats!

Dogs lick themselves, too, but much less often than cats. Dogs' smooth tongues lack the spines that make cats' tongues a great grooming tool. That's why dogs can use a little help from their owners to get squeaky clean.

# Who's the most athletic?

Cats are great climbers. They love to perch in trees, on refrigerators, and even on rooftops. They can jump long distances and almost always land on their feet.

**WINNER: tie!**

Still, when it comes to going the distance, dogs are hard to beat. Some breeds are able to run or work all day. Sled dogs in the famous Iditarod race run 1,110 miles through the Alaskan wilderness.

Both dogs and cats are capable of outstanding physical feats. They just have different talents.

Alaskan Iditarod race

**WINNER: dogs!**

## Who's the most social?

Most dogs like to hang out with other dogs. This trait was passed down from wolves, which live in packs. Many dog owners take their dogs to places where they can have active social lives.

**weird but true**

There are dog parks, doggie restaurants, and even hotels for dogs!

Most cats are loners. In order to get along, cats usually have to be raised together. Cats might like to cuddle with their favorite humans, but they leave the pet parties to the dogs.

# Final Showdown

## Who comes in the greatest number of shapes and sizes?

Cats haven't changed much from their wild ancestors. Scientists think cats started living with humans about 9,000 years ago. Cats were useful for catching pests that raided food supplies.

Today, there are about 80 breeds of cats. The biggest difference among cat breeds is in the length, color, and feel of their coats.

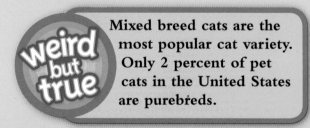

weird but true

Mixed breed cats are the most popular cat variety. Only 2 percent of pet cats in the United States are purebreds.

Persian

sphynx

Maine coon

Siamese

greyhound

beagle

Yorkshire terrier

miniature poodle

38

More than 15,000 years ago, humans and wolves started living together side by side. Eventually, humans tamed the pups into the world's first domesticated animal—the dog.

Over the years, people have bred dogs for specific tasks like guarding, herding, and companionship. The result: dogs of all different shapes and sizes. There are more than 400 dog breeds recognized around the world.

WINNER: dogs!

## Who's the smartest?

Sit. Stay. Roll over! Most dog owners know it's easy to train pups to do tricks. Dogs' brains are wired for obeying a pack leader, so they're happy to listen to their human master's commands.

Dogs can be trained to do all kinds of tasks. They can serve as guide dogs for people who can't see. They can help search for lost people after a disaster. Some dogs even help police officers catch criminals.

Tell a cat to sit, and it will likely give you a look that seems to say, "I don't think so." Some cat owners believe that cats are too smart to take orders from a human.

While dogs have a natural drive to please a leader, cats generally do not. But they can still be trained to do tricks. Using tasty food rewards, experienced trainers can make cats jump through hoops, fetch toys, and give high fives.

**WINNER: tie!**

**weird but true**

Cats can learn to use the toilet instead of a litter box—and flush afterward!

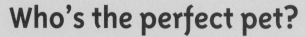

## Who's the perfect pet?

So which animal makes the best pet? Dogs and cats have different traits that have developed over thousands of years. Your dog might chew up your favorite pair of shoes. Your cat might ignore you when you call its name. But most dogs and cats love their owners even when they're not on their best behavior.

When a cat curls
up on your lap, or
a dog gives you
a sloppy lick of
affection, you'll
know who the
perfect pet is.
Whichever one
you own!

**WINNER: tie!**

# Glossary

**CANINE:** A group of meat-eating mammals that includes the domestic dog, wolf, fox, jackal, and coyote

**DOMESTICATED:** The condition of an animal, changed from being wild to living closely with humans

**EVOLVE:** To change or develop naturally over long periods of time

**INSTINCT:** Behavior that animals are born knowing how to do

**PACK:** A group of canines that lives and hunts together

**CARNIVORE:** An animal that eats other animals

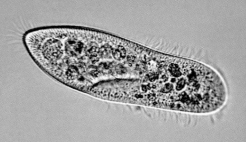

**CELL:** The basic building block of a living thing. Large plants and animals are made up of trillions of cells.

**FELINE:** A group of meat-eating mammals that includes the domestic cat, lion, tiger, lynx, and cheetah

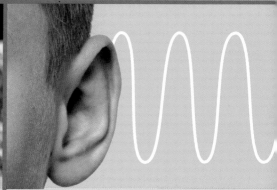

**HERTZ:** A unit of measurement for sound

**PREDATOR:** An animal that hunts other animals for food

**PROTEIN:** A nutrient in meat that is an important part of all living things.

# Index